10 Esser
Business Growth Strategies

That Your Competitors
Don't Want You To Know About

10 simple strategies that will rapidly
grow your business to whatever size
you want it to be!

BDA

Business Development Advisors

www.businessdevelopmentadvisors.co.uk

10 Essential
Business Growth Strategies

That Your Competitors Don't Want You To Know About

Printed and bound by MPG Biddles Ltd, King's Lynn, Norfolk.

Designed and Published By Blessings Book Publishing All Rights Reserved
www.theblessingsbook.com/publishing

Contents

Introduction...4

Strategy 1: The Business Plan.................................7

Strategy 2: The Marketing Plan 11

Strategy 3: Marketing Fundamentals....................18

Strategy 4: The Principles of Business Growth 26

Strategy 5: Referral Marketing 36

Strategy 6: Low Cost Marketing 45

Strategy 7: The Internet 54

Strategy 8: Copywriting 60

Strategy 9: Direct Mail..........................71

Strategy 10: Information Products 77

Webliography... 87

Introduction

10 Essential Business Growth Strategies That Your Competitors Don't Want You To Know About is designed to demonstrate to small business owners that by employing a few simple tried and tested strategies, growing and developing businesses is actually a relatively simple and logical process as long as you have the right mind set to actually go out and make it happen.

The objective of this book is to show you the steps you need to take to get yourself ready to market your business, to position the business in the right way so that customers want to do business with you and then to guide you through the steps you need to take to make your business everything that you want it to be.

Who is this book aimed at?

While the principals which will be discussed are universal, it will have particular relevance to:

▶ Owners and directors of SMEs

▶ Small company marketing managers

▶ One man bands

▶ Professional advisors and consultants

When people talk about business growth and business development, what they really want is more profit. As the old adage goes "Turnover is vanity, profit is sanity". While at the big corporate level there may be reasons why turnover is desirable as an end in itself, at the SME level it is all about profit and while there may be plenty of ways a business can increase profit, in most instances and for the sake of this book, we are going to look at ways which grow the business – both turnover and profit – and to do that we are going to focus on growth through marketing.

What is this marketing thing?

Marketing is a term which is used very widely and often inaccurately by people who should know better. There are any number of definitions of marketing but The Chartered Institute of Marketing's definition sums it up quite concisely:

66 The management process responsible for
identifying, anticipating and satisfying
customer requirements profitably. 99

The thing is that you can have the best product in the world, but if your potential customers don't know about it, the benefits it will deliver to them and how they can get hold of it, then you're not going to sell anything and someone else who may have an inferior offering but better marketing may clean up.

As Peter Drucker, the famous American writer and management consultant said:

66 Because its purpose is to create a customer, the business
has two – and only two – functions;
marketing and innovation.
Marketing and innovation produce results,
all the rest are costs. 99

Information Based Marketing

We live in an age of information overload. Whether that be through modern technology based media such as the internet, which can now be accessed in any number of ways or through more traditional channels such as TV, radio, newspapers etc, we are continually surrounded by massive amounts of information. This has created very savvy consumers, who want to make their own decisions based on factual information as opposed to being sold to by silver tongued salesmen. For this reason, to make sales you need to be providing the information that customers want. This is called information based marketing and really is selling without selling, if you get what I mean.

The more information you give to today's highly educated consumer the better. You then take on the role of the trustworthy educator, someone who isn't trying to sell but is providing them with all the information they need to make their own educated decision. The sense of trust and security which is engendered in this way means that you are more likely to be the supplier they select.

selling without selling

Strategy 1: The Business Plan

We've all heard about business plans but what exactly is a business plan, who should have one and why will it help you?

A business plan is a formal statement of what you are planning to achieve in your business and contains the background to your business and your industry, how you're going to achieve the objectives you've set yourself, the timescales involved i.e. when you're going to do it, who's going to be involved and the financial side of things – how much money you plan to make, how much you're going to spend and how you're going to manage your cash flow.

Who Needs A Business Plan?

A lot of people think that businesses only need a business plan when they are starting up. Now it's true that a business plan is vital to new businesses but it is also true that all businesses should have a plan. The process of sitting down and deciding where you want the business to go over the next period of time should focus your mind on what needs to be done and how you are going to do it. Having a business plan will not guarantee your success but it certainly kicks you off on the right foot. Many business owners are so involved in the day to day running of their business that they never take the time to sit back, take an objective view and actually plan the what, how, when and how much of their business.

The companies who really need a business plan the most are those who are looking to raise finance. Start up companies are the most likely to be looking for finance but any company who is looking to expand may need to generate money to fund the expansion. In these instances all elements of the plan will be important but the turnover and cash flow sections will be absolutely vital.

What Should You Include In The Plan?

Your business plan doesn't need to become War and Peace. No one's going to be impressed just because it contains a lot of pages. However there are certain headings that you will definitely need to include.

▶ **Executive Summary**: the executive summary is really just a distillation of all the key elements of the plan. It may well be just one side of paper. When your plan is being read by investors or lenders they will start with the executive summary, so it needs to contain the key points.

▶ **Business Description**: in this section you will lay out your vision for the business. What you do, who your customers will be, where you will operate, the reasons why you will be successful and the market you will be selling into.

If you're an established business you will describe your progress in terms of turnover and customers and any plans you have for the future.

▶ **Competitive Analysis**: unfortunately none of us are the only operators in our sector. We all have competitors. You should identify key competitors within your area of operation, their strengths and weaknesses and indicate how you believe you will be able to compete against them. At the end of the day how you approach the competitive threat will determine how successful you will be.

▶ **Market Analysis**: whether there is a demand for your product will be absolutely fundamental to the success of your business. Within the market analysis you should review the total market which you are operating in, looking at the dynamics and trends within that market. You should then refine it down to focus in on the state of the market within your specific area.

▶ **Marketing and Sales Plan**: marketing, as we have already discussed, is absolutely vital for your business' success. This part of the plan will be a distillation of your marketing plan which we will discuss later. It will outline how you will promote and sell to your customers, who your customers are, how you'll communicate with them, how you'll price your products and how you'll promote them.

▶ **Your Team**: if you're looking for investment, the skills and experience of your team, both management and staff, will be very important. Investors will want to know that there are the relevant skills within your business to deliver your plan.

If you're writing the plan more for personal consumption, this exercise can focus your mind on whether you have the right personnel with the right skills in the right roles.

▶ **Your Operations Plan**: this section will cover all the operational issues – details about your location and its suitability to your operation, whether you own or lease your premises and any alterations or investment you may need to make.

Management information and IT systems and any upgrades or changes will be relevant within this part of the plan.

You should also describe how personnel within the company is organised i.e. if you have a field structure or a production team and the reporting lines.

▶ **Financials**: we all know that the world is run by accountants, so the financial part of the plan is the section which determines the success or failure of the business.

Of course the next twelve months' figures are the most important elements of the plan but it's good discipline to do a three year plan.

Your financial plan should include:

Sales forecast showing how much you are going to turnover and at what margin.

Cash flow forecast which will demonstrate that the business will generate enough cash at the right time to cover the business' needs.

Profit and loss forecast to identify the profit you will make after all costs and overheads have been deducted.

Strategy 2: The Marketing Plan

You're now clear on why you need a business plan and what you're going to put in it. As we said one of the constituent parts is the marketing plan.

While the business plan tells you where you want to take your business, the marketing plan is the element which is actually going to do the work to get you there.

Again your marketing plan doesn't need to be a huge document. In fact if it's too large you're probably less likely to use it. So make sure it's written in such a way that you will use it regularly.

Objectives

The very first part of your marketing plan has to be your marketing objectives. Before you start you have to know what you want to achieve. If you don't do that how will you know if you're being successful or not?

Your objectives are likely to include:

▶ Your turnover for the coming year

▶ Your margin and profit

▶ The number of leads you intend to generate

▶ The number of new customers you're planning to win

▶ The number of customers you expect to lose

▶ Your average transaction value

Market Research

To be successful in any market you have to understand it :

▶ What are the key drivers in the market?

▶ Who are the major players/competitors within the area of your operation?

▶ What are the trends within the market?

Only when you understand the market will you know the important issues, what the market is looking for and how to fulfil that need.

So How Do You Do Your Research?

One source is the general published information which is out in the public domain. This will give you generalised information.

For information on your competitors, the best sources are their web sites, suppliers and even customers.

Another way to get really useful information is by doing the research yourself.

1. **Your Existing Customers:** you can simply ask them what they want, what issues they perceive in the market and what are the key issues from their point of view. Hopefully their responses will tie in with the service you are providing for them.

2. **Past Customers:** you can ask exactly the same questions of past customers, assuming you're still on friendly terms with them. The benefit of asking them what they want is that it potentially gives you the opportunity to rekindle the relationship.

3. **Non Customers:** again the questions will be the same but it allows you to introduce your company and possibly sow the first seeds of a relationship.

Internal and External Analysis

In order to understand your business environment and where your business sits within it, as well as research there are a couple of other tools you can use.

The first of these is a **PEST** analysis:

Political and legal issues and changes which affect your market place.

Economic influences such as the state of the economy, interest rates, consumer confidence etc.

Social issues which will have an impact on you – changing demographics, fashions and lifestyles.

Technology – the most obvious of these is the internet and how it is changing almost all markets.

The other tool which will be useful to you at this stage is a **SWOT** analysis.

Strengths: these are the areas that your business is good at, the areas where you excel.

Weaknesses: the reason for identifying the areas of weakness is so that you can take action to improve these areas.

Opportunities: what areas are you currently not exploiting to the maximum which with a bit of focus your business could capitalise on?

Threats: what issues are there which could endanger your business either now or in the near future?

In the same way that you should produce a new marketing plan each year, you should revisit your PEST and SWOT analyses every year to see whether the issues have changed and to identify whether your business has moved forward.

Identify Your Audiences

One of the greatest mistakes a business can make is not to identify specific niche audiences and instead to market their products to everyone.

To decide on your target market(s) you must identify people/companies who:

1. Need or want what you supply
2. Can afford to pay what you charge
3. Have similarities which enable you to group them together
4. Can be reached at a realistic price by your marketing communications

The issue people have is that by identifying specific niche audiences, they are worried that they will be limiting the universe who might potentially buy their products. The answer to this is yes of course you will be limiting your audience but by targeting those groups who meet the criteria above and by tailoring your message to them directly, your conversion rate will be dramatically higher and your marketing costs will be significantly lower.

The key issue here is relevance. For someone to choose to do business with you, your product or service has to be relevant to them and with the best will in the world, unless you're Coca Cola you cannot be relevant to everyone.

So once you have identified who are your best niche audiences, you can now start to tailor both your product and your marketing to make them directly relevant to these audiences. What we are talking about here is the difference between a rifle and a shot gun. A rifle targets its victim precisely and delivers a knockout blow while the shot gun sprays pellets around with lots missing their target.

REMEMBER: YOU MUST IDENTIFY YOUR TARGET AUDIENCE BEFORE YOU SPEND TIME AND MONEY ON MARKETING

Pricing

Deciding how to price your product or service is an absolutely fundamental and vital part of your marketing plan.

There are several factors which will influence your pricing decisions:

▶ Your positioning–are you planning to market yourself as up-market, mid-market or down-market?

▶ How much competition is there locally? How easy is it for customers to get your product elsewhere?

▶ Is your product one that can be compared directly?

There are two basic calculations you can do to arrive at your pricing:

1. Research the market to identify what the same/similar products sell for locally and then applying the factors above.
2. Taking your cost price and simply adding on a specific percentage. This approach is obviously not tailored to the dictates of the market and so is likely to be rather hit and miss.

Geographical Area

The area you will operate in will be dictated by the nature of your business. If you're an online business, you may trade globally while if you're a retail outlet your catchment area may be only a few miles.

Generally speaking, the more local your customers are, the easier and cheaper it is to service them, whether that be delivery costs or if you actually visit them.

The purpose of defining your target area will be to allow you to identify the most appropriate marketing and communication channels.

Whatever the nature of your business, it's worth remembering that the larger your area of operation, the thinner your marketing communications are likely to be spread.

Promotional Channels

Once you have the elements of your promotional proposition in place, you have to decide the most appropriate, effective and cost effective ways to communicate your message. In order to give yourself an overview of your year's activity, you should plan each campaign out on a spreadsheet with the activity on the vertical axis and the months on the horizontal.

At the planning stage this doesn't have to be absolutely precise.

For example you may plan to use Google Adwords all year, so you would just blank out all twelve months but intend to run a couple of e-marketing and direct mail campaigns for a month or two. In this situation you would just indicate those months when you plan the activity to happen.

Budget

Assuming that your marketing is working and generating additional business, you should budget as much as you can for your marketing spend.

If you spend £100 and only make £50 profit, that is a cost. However if you spend £100 and make £500 or £1000 profit, that is an investment.

On the spreadsheet you set up to plan your marketing communications, you should open another tab to manage your marketing expenditure.

For each piece of activity you should have three different columns. One for the budgeted cost, one for the actual cost and one for the variance.

This way on a month by month basis you can track your expenditure and make sure that you are in control of exactly how much you spend.

Strategy 3: Marketing Fundamentals

Now you've got both your business plan and your marketing plan in place, there is one more element of planning you need to do. I call this next stage your "Marketing Fundamentals." Before you go out and start actively promoting your business in the market place, you have to ensure that you are presenting your best face, that you are making your business as attractive as possible to potential customers and that you are making it easy for prospects to decide to do business with you. These fundamental building blocks will ensure that your marketing and promotional efforts have the best chance of success.

Define Your Proposition

When anyone sets up a business, we know what it is we are going to do and what we're going to sell. Now it's all very well for us to know but do your prospective customers know what it is you do and more importantly do you communicate it in terms which resonate with your customers?

An example of this would be a bank.

When asked what he does a banker might say:

66 I lend money to my customers. 99

However in the customer's language that might translate into:

> **66**The bank provides me with the money to buy more equipment and so expand my business.**99**

A courier service might say:

> **66**We deliver parcels.**99**

whereas from his customer's point of view:

> **66**They enable me to fulfil customer orders by supplying my products to my customers.**99**

You see the difference?

So you need to develop a short, pithy sentence which sums up what you do, so that when you're asked what business you're in, you can answer in a way that is immediately relevant and understood by a potential customer.

This sentence can then be used on your web site and any other corporate materials you may produce.

Market Positioning

When we decide to buy something, we normally have a good idea about the sort of quality we are looking for and also roughly the amount we are prepared to pay.

If you want to buy a coat but you've only got £10 you'll probably head to your local charity shop or maybe a market stall. However if you want to buy a coat and are planning to spend £1000, instead of the charity shop you might decide to go to Harrods.

So how do we make these decisions? We make the decisions based on our knowledge of the positioning of the different outlets. Everything about these outlets including their location, the store decor and their corporate identity (if they have one) down to the quality of their carrier bags reinforce their positioning within the market.

The benefit of this from the consumer's point of view is that we have an accurate idea of where to go to meet our specific needs.

You need to apply the same logic to your business. You need to communicate your positioning within the market to potential customers so that you attract those for whom the quality and pricing of your product or service meets their needs.

So do you want to position your business at the Harrods end of the spectrum or are you more of a charity shop kind of business? No one positioning is better than the other but you must ensure that if you position yourself as Harrods and charge accordingly, all aspects of your business live up to that promise.

Features And Benefits

A classic mistake that so many businesses make is to give their customers a long list of all the features of their product and then are surprised when they don't make a sale. What these businesses are forgetting is that we don't buy features, we buy benefits.

We buy it because we are motivated by WIIFM or *What's In It For Me*. We buy products for what they do for us – the benefits.

No one buys a chair because it is ergonomically designed. No, I buy it because it supports my back and is really comfortable. I don't buy the chair because it is treated with stain retardant but because when I spill my coffee on it, the liquid runs off and doesn't stain the fabric.

So all business owners should look at their business and make a list of all the features of whatever it is they sell. Then on the other side of the paper list all the benefits and the advantages they deliver to the owner.

If you struggle with converting features to benefits you can use the expression:

66...which means that...99

This camera has a resolution of 10 megapixels. So what, I haven't a clue what 1 megapixel is so why would I need 10?

This camera has a resolution of 10 megapixels which means that your pictures will be exceedingly sharp with great depth of colour. OK, now I know what you're talking about, I'll have one.

Once you've identified the benefits of your product, you can use them in all your sales collateral, on your website or wherever you're trying to sell your product.

Unique Selling Point

These days most people are aware of the expression USP or unique selling point but maybe aren't so clear about exactly what it is and why they should have one.

A unique selling point, exactly as it sounds, is some unique characteristic of your business which makes you different and in the eyes of your customers, better than your competitors.

Say I'm looking to buy a tent to go camping with and say I'm a very organised sort of person and I do lots of research on half a dozen tents. Now all the tents are pretty similar – they all sleep two people, they're all waterproof, they all cost about the same but one of them folds up much smaller than the others and is very light(I'm making this example up by the way.) Now the size and weight are very important to me as I'll be carrying the tent in a backpack.

Suddenly the choice has become obvious.

Ideally what you want is when your customers do their product comparisons, there is something about your product (the USP) which makes it stand out and makes the decision a "no brainer."

Now if you don't have a USP, you know what can happen.

I'm still very organised and before making my decision I do my research and I list all the features (and hopefully benefits) of the competing items but there really is nothing to choose between them. So what am I going to do? That's right I'm going to choose the cheapest.

Now this is an area that most of us don't want to get involved in – a lowest price auction – unless of course your USP is that you have the lowest price. There are lots of examples of companies using low prices as their USP but it is fraught with danger. There's always going to be someone who has managed to source product more cheaply or for whatever reason is prepared to slash their prices. So where does this leave you? To maintain your USP you now have to cut your price and therefore reduce your margin and before you know it you're not making any money.

So you need to ask yourself what is there about your business which gives it stand out, which would make it the obvious choice in a beauty parade.

If the answer is nothing then you need to do something about that.

There are a number of ways in which you can address this:

1. Analyse your business in depth. When you really look at it there may be an aspect which can be majored on which contains a genuine customer benefit that none of your competitors offer.
2. When you do your analysis you may find an element of your business which is common in your industry but which none of your competitors focus on. Although it is not unique to you, if you start to present it as a major benefit, your customers will perceive it as unique and reward you with their custom.

There is a classic example of this from the 1920's in the US:

> At the time Schlitz was just another brand of beer until they hit on the idea of telling customers about their production processes – how they went through thousands of tests to find the best and richest tasting yeast, how they distilled their water three separate times to ensure its purity and how they steam sterilised the bottles. Although all their competitors went through the same process, no one actually told their customers. So Schlitz started to communicate this information which then in the minds of their customers gave them a unique selling point and moved them from being the sixth largest selling beer to being the number one.

3. Re-engineer your business to provide an aspect or service that no one else offers. While this may seem a bit extreme, if it can make you stand out above your competitors as offering a better product, the results will make the effort more than worthwhile.

Risk Reversal

Have you ever wondered why a prospect who you thought was just about to buy from you, eventually decides not to?

There could be a number of reasons, but the most common one is that the prospect perceives that buying your product exposes him to some kind of risk.

Perhaps your product may not do what it says it will, that he might just not get on with it, that he may be paying too much for it, that it won't be comfortable etc, etc. The list goes on and on. Now if you can find a way to remove all the risk from the buyer then it is much easier for him to say yes.

So how can you remove the risk for the buyer?

There are two very common and successful ways of doing it.

1. Free Trial

The customer can trial the product for 30 days in their own home or office. If they don't like it they can just return it for a full refund. This overcomes so many of the standard objections.

The Hi Fi company Bose often offer 30 day trials of their music systems. This is perfect because different locations often have different acoustics. What sounds great in one location may not sound so good elsewhere. So not surprisingly customers may be nervous about buying a system. A home trial gives them the opportunity to test it for themselves so that they know definitively whether it is the right product for them before they have to commit to the purchase.

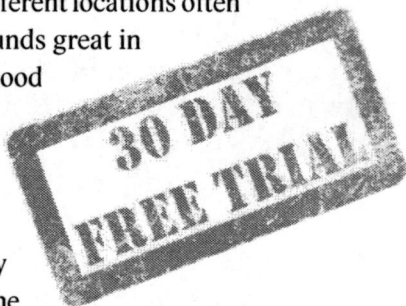

The other great thing about this risk removal method is that inertia often steps in. Once customers have something on trial at home, they often never get round to returning it.

2. The Money Back Guarantee

If you offer a money back guarantee, you are demonstrating to your customers that you are totally confident in your product. From the customer's point of view all the risk is removed. If for whatever reason they're not absolutely happy with the product, they can get their money back so there's absolutely no reason not to buy.

One of my first clients was a servicing garage. All garages suffer from the perception that they might be crooks because most of us have no idea what goes on under the bonnet. When I first suggested the idea of offering a guarantee in which if the customer wasn't happy with any aspect of the service, they would receive a 100% refund, the garage owner was horrified. It was such a radical idea in that business and he felt he would be very exposed to customer fraud.

Eventually he came round to the idea. Just think what a message of quality and openness it sent out to customers. By advertising the guarantee in the local paper, he immediately differentiated his garage from all his competitors and gave himself a powerful USP. Within two months the number of cars he was servicing increased by 28% and he was having to take on additional staff.

Many business owners react as my garage client did and are worried that customers will rip them off. The fact is that one or two might but most people are fundamentally honest. However, if you have to refund one or two unscrupulous customers, that may just be the price you pay for the scores of new customers you have generated.

Strategy 4: The Principles of Business Growth

So now you should have the fundamental aspects of your business proposition in place. These will ensure that your business is positioned in the most favourable light to your prospective customers and you are making it as easy as possible for them to decide to do business with you.

You're now thinking of getting on and doing some marketing, but there are a few basic principals which you need to be aware of before you start .

A Multi Channel Approach

Most business owners are aware that they need to do some marketing, to get themselves out there and put their proposition in front of prospective customers. However if you asked them what marketing they actually do, classic answers would be:

> 66 We advertise regularly in the local paper 99

> 66 I go to my local networking group every week 99

> 66 We have a girl who does telemarketing for us 99

The great majority of businesses rely on one channel to communicate their marketing messages. This is a very dangerous strategy.

If the advertisement that you've been running for ages stops working, it may take you a few weeks to realise it is no longer delivering the number of leads you need. It will then take you a while to create a new advert. This could mean that for several weeks you have no business generating activity happening. Having no new business coming in for several weeks could be disastrous for you while being a godsend to your competitors.

A few years ago I was working with a decent sized business who relied on a direct sales force of 4 salesmen. By their own admission 3 of them weren't very good and then the one good one left. They were suddenly left with no effective way to bring in the orders.

Instead of putting all your eggs in one basket, it is very much more effective to use a multi channel approach. There are loads of different channels you can use, you just have to select the ones that are right for your business.

Examples of marketing channels:

Advertising	Exhibitions	Promotions
Article Marketing	Internet Marketing	Referral Marketing
Direct Mail	Joint Ventures	Search Engine Optimisation (SEO)
Direct Sales	Networking	Social Media
E-marketing	PR	Telemarketing

The benefit of this approach is that if one channel stops working for you, the other channels will continue to generate business, while you make corrections to the channel which is no longer working effectively.

The other benefit of a multi channel approach is when one channel backs up and reinforces another.

For example if you mount a direct marketing campaign and send out a load of letters, your response will determined by a number of factors

- ☐ The quality of the mailing list
- ☐ The accuracy of the targeting
- ☐ The quality of your copywriting
- ☐ The offer you make

However, the rule of thumb states that you are likely to get somewhere between 0.5% – 2.5% response rate. The other variable which will influence the response will be your follow up.

If the day after you send out the letters, you send an email, referring back to the letter and distilling the key points, you may well double your response. If the day after that you follow up with some telemarketing, you should be able to double or triple your response again.

Testing And Assessing

FACT: Marketing can be expensive

Bad marketing is a cost to the business, while good marketing is a wise investment which repays its cost many times over.

Who knows whether your marketing is good or bad? Well I certainly hope that you do. Not knowing whether your marketing is working or not is just stupid.

Marketing doesn't have to be an art – it can and should be a science.

The first thing to do is to calculate your immediate return from a marketing campaign. It doesn't matter what form that campaign takes – whether it be e-marketing, Google Adwords or something more traditional such as advertising or direct mail. You know what you've spent on the campaign and you should be able to track what business comes in as a direct result. This will only cover your immediate return because at this stage you cannot know how much repeat business you might receive.

Now the question is if I run a campaign and get some response, how do I know if some of that would have happened anyway?

The answer is to identify the campaign in some way. Maybe you could ask for response on a dedicated phone number or you could tell customers to quote a particular reference when responding.

In this way you can track exactly what response you're getting and whether your marketing is working for you or not.

The other thing you should be doing is testing different elements of your campaign against each other.

Small tweaks to a headline can double response rates. Changing your pricing can have surprising results. Sometimes putting your prices up by 50% can put your response rate up by 50%.

Testing should become an ingrained habit. Even when you have a great response, that should become your benchmark which you strive to beat.

A business which is continually testing is a business which is honing its marketing efficiency.

Regularity Of Contact: The Irresistible Customer Relationship Model

People's wants and needs change constantly as their circumstances change. What I want today may no longer be relevant tomorrow.

A "No" from a prospect, while it says "I'm not going to take up your offer today" could be a simple way of saying any number of things:

▶ I haven't got enough information to make a decision

▶ I haven't got enough money this month to buy from you

▶ I haven't got time to think about it properly right now

None of these are a definitive "No." They are all saying not today, but by next month or the following month their circumstances may have changed and they may be ready to say "Yes".

To be successful with your marketing, you have to be persistent. Innumerable studies have shown that it may take up to seven points of contact or "touches" before someone responds. If each time you contact your prospect, you give them another reason to buy from you, eventually you should have either overcome all their objections or hit them at just the moment when they are ready to buy. The other point here relates back to the idea of multiple channels. If you use different contact mechanisms to vary your offer and build on the previous contacts, your persistence will pay off with dramatic results.

Lifetime Value

What is lifetime value? Put simply and not surprisingly, it is a calculation of how much a customer is worth to you over the total lifetime that they do business with you.

It's very easy to look at marketing activity in the short term.

Say you do a marketing campaign which costs you £3000. From this activity you generate 100 customers who each spend £60 with you.

So you have generated £6000. Now let's say that your margin is 50%. So in total you have generated £3000 of profit.

Now this sounds like a complete waste of time doesn't it? You've spent £3000 and generated £3000. On top of that there is all the time and effort you put in.

Now hold on a moment. If these 100 customers become regular customers and spend £60 four times per year and continue to buy from you for 5 years, the sums suddenly look very different.

100 x £60 x 4x per year x 5 years.

Suddenly we have £120,000 of turnover x 50% margin = £60,000 of gross profit.

Not so shabby.

But hold on, there's more.

What if each of these customers were to give you 1 referral, who each buy exactly the same amount from you.

Now you've got another £60,000 in your pocket.

Perhaps that £3000 expenditure wasn't such a bad idea after all.

So why is it important to know the lifetime value of your customers?

The answer is that until you understand how much a customer is worth to you, you don't know how much you should spend acquiring that customer.

If a customer's lifetime value to you is £20 you may consider spending 50p or maybe £1 acquiring him or her.

But if the customer is worth £200 or even £2000 to you, you're going to be prepared to spend much more getting the customer in the first place.

Concentrate On All Drivers

If you're looking to grow your business, there are only a few ways to do it:

1. Generate new customers
2. Increase the number of transactions from your existing customers
3. Grow the average transaction value
4. Increase your margins
5. Hold on to your customers for longer

So which of these is the most important? That's impossible to say as they are all important.

If you want to grow your business, we've now agreed that you need to grow these key drivers. Growing any one of these by, let's say 10%, will be good for your business. But if you can manage to grow them all 10% the effect will be dramatic.

Let's have a look at an example:

Number of Leads		Conversion Rate		Number of Transactions		Transaction Value		Margin		Buying Lifetime
100	×	20% = 20 sales	×	3 = 60 sales	×	£50 = £3000	×	50% = £1500	×	4 Years = £6000

Now we'll increase each driver by 10%

Number of Leads		Conversion Rate		Number of Transactions		Transaction Value		Margin		Buying Lifetime
110	×	22% = 24.2 sales	×	3.3 = 79.8 sales	×	£55 = £4389	×	55% = £2414	×	4.4 Years = £10621

This equates to a massive 77% increase in profit.

The Need For Promotion

When you are looking to grow your business, new customers are always going to be a key ingredient. In all businesses there is a natural churn as customers change their buying habits, move away or even get lured away so you will need to be continuously feeding in new customers at the front end.

We'll assume now that you have your marketing fundamentals in place and that you've decided how you're going to communicate your proposition to your target audience. But is this going to be enough? Well it may be but a lot of customers procrastinate.

So you need to do something to force them to make the decision to buy from you. And the way to do that is through promotions and special offers.

The classic special offer is the discount – 33% off or Save £50.

But there are lots of ways discounts can be expressed:

- ► Buy one get one free
- ► Buy one get one half price
- ► 3 for 2
- ► 33% extra free

Or for a different sort of market:

- ☐ I month free
- ☐ Free consultation
- ☐ Free special report
- ☐ Free business analysis

The classic complaint about this sort of offer is that if I give my product away at this level of discount, I won't make much money. This may be the case. But that may be the price of getting a new customer. While you might make a reduced margin on this first transaction, it gives you the opportunity to start building a long lasting relationship and the opportunity to make money down the line.

If your business is about one-off sales, then you are going to have to look very carefully at the level of incentive you give away. But for businesses with repeat sales, you should take a slightly longer term view and do whatever it takes to start trading with new customers.

Make Sure You Have A Back End

So what's a back end I hear you ask?

A back end is having additional products ready to sell to your customers immediately after they have bought from you the first time.

While your very first sale will have the costs of generating that customer associated with it, your back end products will be at full margin.

The back end can often be a product linked directly to the first purchase. When you buy a pair of shoes, how often are you offered the stain resistant spray? When you buy electrical goods, you know they're going to try to sell you the extended warranty.

If you haven't got an obviously linked product to sell, find something else that will appeal to this audience. Remember they have recently made the decision to buy from you and assuming that you have given them great service they will be very positively disposed towards you. So when you approach them with another great product, your uptake will be rewardingly high.

Strategy 5: Referral Marketing

We're now starting to get to the exciting part of the book. Our marketing fundamentals are in place and we've got our heads around a few basic principles of business development. So now we're ready to start marketing the business.

When the subject of marketing comes up, most business owners start worrying about cost. But marketing doesn't have to cost much, in fact there are lots of things you can do which don't cost anything at all.

The first of these low cost marketing channels we're going to talk about is Referral Marketing.

It is estimated that small businesses generate nearly 90% of their new business via referrals.

What Is A Referral?

Referrals are the recommendations that existing customers give to people looking for whatever it is that you provide. Most people would just call it "word of mouth".

There are several reasons why referrals are so good:

1. Someone recommended to your business by someone they trust is extremely likely to do business with you.
2. They build your business with little effort or cost to you.
3. They are an endorsement of your business – a referral confirms that a customer is so happy with your service that they are prepared to put their own reputation on the line by recommending you.
4. They provide you with the highest margin business as the cost of acquisition is so low.
5. Referrals make you feel good about your business.

When asked how they generate their business, most SMEs will mention "word of mouth" as one of their primary sources. Now this is absolutely fine except that normally "word of mouth" is a completely passive activity.

You do not have any influence over the quantity or timing of referrals. If someone happens to ask one of your customers for a recommendation, you may get referred but if no one actively asks, it doesn't happen.

So what you need to do is to make referral marketing an active part of your marketing strategy, so that you maximise the quantity and control the timing.

So how do you go about encouraging your customers to refer you to their contacts?

There are five key elements involved in your referral marketing strategy:

1. You must create a referral marketing plan.
2. You need to develop a referral marketing mindset.
3. Your referral rating – you have to make sure that your business is worthy of being recommended.
4. A strategic customer care programme – you need to ensure you create a very positive impression and that you stay top of your customer's mind.
5. You must implement a proactive referral strategy to encourage your customers to refer you.

Referral Marketing Plan

Your referral marketing plan will be a sub set of your main marketing plan and shouldn't be a long and complex document. But we all know that if we have a plan we are much more likely to perform the task than if we don't.

Your plan should basically look at who, how and when.

- ✓ Who are you going to talk to?
- ✓ How are you going to approach them?
- ✓ When are you going to do it?

In addition to these elements you should also set targets of what you hope to achieve from your referral marketing activities. How many new customers do you want to generate and how much income do you plan to raise?

The final point you need to consider within your plan is the budget. While referral marketing can be completely free, you may want to allocate some money for communication with your customers or for rewards for actually referring you.

Develop A Referral Mindset

Why would someone refer you or your business to someone else?

The only reason is because they have been impressed with your business and based on this they believe you will also provide a good service to their contact. This means to be referable you have to be committed to providing outstanding customer service at all times. If someone is referred to your business but is unimpressed with the service you provide, not only will you not do business with them again, but it is also likely that you may lose the business of the initial referrer, as he has put his reputation on the line by referring you in the first place. As part of your referral mindset you should always remember that each customer has their own network of customers. So when you serve that customer, you are in effect potentially opening the door to all his contacts.

Of course some of your customers will have larger networks than others which will give them a higher referral value to you. You must identify those with the higher referral values and make sure that you pay them extra special attention.

The last point to note is that the referral mindset applies to all members of staff. Everyone within the company will have their own network of contacts and therefore of potential customers. If everyone therefore is constantly aware of the benefits of referrals and keeps the single minded commitment to customer service, then your potential for referrals is dramatically increased.

Your Referral Rating

At the risk of stating the obvious, to get referrals, you have to be referable.

What does it take to be referable? To be honest it's not rocket science. You must be:

- ✓ Credible
- ✓ Reliable
- ✓ Have integrity
- ✓ A sound reputation
- ✓ A track record of success

In addition to these you must be skilled in relationship building. So much of business comes down to relationships – you need to be someone people like dealing with and who they can rely on to solve their particular business problems and who they also feel motivated to help. But the base line is that the key issue will be the quality of the service you provide to your customers.

If you continuously focus on your customers' needs and exceeding their expectations, your referral rating will be high and the number of referrals you get will be correspondingly high.

A Strategic Customer Care Progamme

As we've now established, referrals stem from happy customers so it's up to you to make sure that your customers are not just happy but delighted by you. To go this extra mile you are going to have to do more than just do your job well. You are going to need a detailed customer care programme to make your customers really love you.

▶ Trained and motivated staff will make all the difference between a good service and an exceptional one. Not only do you need your staff to be technically competent but they also need to be friendly, polite and as focused on your customers as you are.

▶ A customer charter will state publicly the levels of service that you are committed to achieving and will demonstrate your focus on your customers. However having published your charter, you need to live up to it, otherwise you will end up shooting yourselves in the foot.

▶ We covered the issue of an official guarantee in the Marketing Fundamentals section, but it is another element which should set your business apart. A guarantee gives your customers total peace of mind and makes them even more confident of referring you.

▶ A formalised complaints procedure gives your customers the reassurance that if something were to go wrong, that they have a channel to air their grievance. It also can work in your favour. If a complaint is speedily and efficiently dealt with, the customer may well be more impressed than if the problem had never arisen.

▶ A customer satisfaction survey enables your customers to give you feedback, both positive and negative. From your point of view you are demonstrating to your customers that you value their opinions and it also allows you to rectify any issues that you may not have been aware of.

▶ Regular customer communication is a vital element of a customer care programme. Your objective is to keep your company top of mind in order to demonstrate your commitment to your customers but also to ensure they select you when they have orders to place.

Referral Strategies

In the same way that there are lots of different closing strategies, there are many ways to generate referrals.

We're just going to deal with a few here.

Strategy 1.

Just ask...

Well that doesn't sound that clever does it? Just ask for a referral. But you'd be amazed how seldom we do it. When did you last ask a customer for a referral?

And why don't we do it? Because we think it might seem pushy. Because we think it might spoil the relationship. Because we just don't feel comfortable doing it and it's easier not to.

I'm not saying that the first time you meet a customer or the first time you do business together that you should ask. As we've already said you have to earn referrals by being referable.

So again it's a five step process to asking for a referral.

a. Firstly you must develop the relationship. No one's going to refer you if you don't get on. So the first thing you must do is build up rapport with your customer.

b. Provide outstanding service – over service the customer. While that might sound expensive and time consuming, if it leads to him referring you on to his network it will be time well spent.

c. Plant referral seeds. What I'm saying here is that when you ask for the referral, it shouldn't come as a surprise to your customer. You should have mentioned before that you will be asking for a referral at some stage. For example when a project has just gone well, just casually mention that you will be looking for a referral later.

d. You must treat the referral request with importance. Don't bring it up in a rush at the end of a meeting or do it in an apologetic, embarrassed manner. By allocating plenty of time to discuss the subject, you position the request as an important business matter.

e. Ask for the referral at the right time. Just after you've provided outstanding service or when you've dug your customer out of a hole and he is feeling seriously indebted to you, is the perfect time to ask. Conversely don't mention the subject when something has just gone wrong. Wait for the right moment before you ask.

Strategy 2

Give to Get...

If you're not very comfortable asking for referrals, the best way to get around that is to give a referral yourself first.

So if you give a customer a referral two things happen. Firstly he is now in the referral mindset and he will be aware of the benefits of referrals. Secondly he will feel indebted to you. You have done him a good turn and he will now be actively looking for a way to reciprocate. So when you now ask him for a referral he should be happy to oblige.

Now it is possible that with the best will in the world he can't think of anyone to refer you to. At this stage you should work with him to profile the kind of referral you're looking for and then make suggestions of the kind of referrals he might be able to make.

Strategy 3

Offer Incentives...

There is absolutely no reason to be embarrassed about your referral plans. The more people who know you are actively seeking referrals, the more who are likely to provide you with them. You should write down your strategy and your plan and then distribute it to everyone who can help you. Within this plan you should stress the reciprocal nature of the plan and position it as a joint business building opportunity.

For some people the clincher will be when you actually offer an incentive or a reward for every referral which actually converts into business. The size of the reward will depend on the nature of your business. If the referral will net you several thousand pounds you can afford to be more generous than if it will just provide a few pounds.

The Process

Once a referral has been made, you need to find out as much information as you can.

▶ How does the referrer know the person to whom you've been referred?

▶ What kind of a business is it?

▶ What position does the prospect hold?

▶ What kind of person is he?

After you've found out as much as you can, the next step is to get the referrer to contact the prospect to tell him about your business and what you can offer him.

Now that the prospect has been primed, you need to contact him the next day while your name is still fresh in his mind.

At this stage, with the sale process underway, you should go back to the referrer and thank him. If everything goes to plan and a sale is made you should find some way to thank both the referrer and your new customer. To take them both out to lunch would be a great way to cement the relationship.

Strategy 6: Low Cost Marketing

Continuing the theme of the last chapter, I repeat – marketing doesn't have to be expensive and I would advise business owners, whether money is tight or in abundant supply, to consider and utilise some of the many low cost or even no cost marketing channels which are available.

Put Your Prices Up

Pricing is a topic worthy of a book all of it's own.

The psychology of pricing is a fascinating and complex issue which I'm not going to go into here.

My point is that the easiest way to grow your profits is to put up your prices. If there are no accompanying overheads, the price rise feeds straight to the bottom line.

Business owners often look horrified when I suggest raising their prices. But the point is most buyers don't buy on price alone. If that was the case there would be no BMWs, Mercedes, Jaguars let alone Rolls Royces on the roads. The fact is we buy on value and the buyers of these cars decide that the value that these cars deliver is worth paying extra for.

So if you have your marketing fundamentals in place then your business does differentiate itself from its competitors and can be seen to deliver value.

Say you charge £1000 for a service, would charging £1050 make that much difference? The answer is in some cases it would and in some it wouldn't.

So you should look at your business and decide whether you offer enough value and are sufficiently differentiated from your competitors to add a little bit to your prices.

Network, Network, Network

We all know the old adage that people do business with people. The more people you know, the more opportunity you have to:

▶ Sell directly to your contacts

▶ Sell to their networks

▶ Get referrals into their networks

These days there are lots of specialist networking groups. BNI is probably the best known but there are lots of them. These groups meet up on a regular basis with the sole intention of making contacts and passing business among the members.

A quick Google search will give you a list of local networking groups.

In addition to these there are other bodies such as the Chambers of Commerce and the Institute of Directors which are good sources of networking opportunities.

Having chosen how you're going to go about your networking, there are a few rules of thumb which will help your networking be more productive.

1. **Commit to attend regularly.** If people see your face regularly it is easier to build relationships and you come over as committed and reliable.

2. **Be a good listener.** Networking isn't a one way street. People will turn off if you talk about yourself continuously. We all know that asking questions and understanding someone else's business is a vital step in the sales process.

3. **Relax.** Networking should be fun. Mix social with business and make some friends.

4. **Realise that networking takes time.** People start recommending you once they've got to know you and to trust you. Therefore you must be prepared to commit to networking as an ongoing commitment.

5. **Rehearse your networking pitch.** When people first meet you, they will ask you what you do. You need to have prepared a brief, benefit filled pitch which sums up what you do in an engaging manner which the listener is likely to remember.

6. **Work the room.** It's too easy when you go networking to talk to the people you know. You must remember the reason for networking is to make new contacts so take yourself out of your comfort zone and introduce yourself to new people. Normally at networking meetings there will be one or two people who seem to know everyone. Make sure you meet these people as they are likely to have the largest networks because of course you're selling as much to their networks as you are to them.

Public Speaking

Speaking in front of an audience isn't everyone's idea of fun but it does present an excellent opportunity to raise both your and your business' profile.

So if you decide it is something you want to pursue there are a number of issues to contend with :

How do you get the opportunity to speak in public?

This is one of those chicken and egg situations. Once you've done an amount of public speaking and you have developed a reputation, you will start to receive invitations to speak and could even be paid for it. To start with, organisations such as the Chambers of Commerce, networking groups, business associations and special interest groups are likely to present the best opportunities.

What should you speak about?

The decision on that will be driven by two considerations:

1. What will your audience be interested in?
2. What do you know about that you can talk authoritatively on?

Once you've decided what to talk about you must consider the situation.

The audience will be focused entirely on you for the duration of your talk. So while this will have the potential to be a fantastic sales opportunity, your presentation must not be an overt sales pitch. You must select a subject matter which is educational and of general interest to your audience. The sales angle comes from you demonstrating your knowledge and expertise and communicating your personality.

You should always schedule a Q and A session at the end as this will allow you to interact with your audience and potentially allow you to open a dialogue with them.

Write Articles

We all dream about the local newspaper or some specialist magazine full of positive information about our company. The problem is that this usually means having to pay for advertising. What adds insult to injury is that when the audience reads our advertisements they often do so with a slightly jaundiced mind set as they know they're being sold to.

A much better idea is to get free exposure by having articles published.

The first step is to decide on a topic which will be of general interest to the readership. Once you've done that you should contact the editor or business editor of the publication to sell in the idea and to check that they also think your idea is right for their audience.

If unfortunately they are not interested, you can try and see whether there is anything else you could write about for them.

With regard to the subject matter, if your article is just an excuse to blow your own trumpet it won't get published. Instead you should choose a topic on which you have real expertise and insight. The benefit to you will accrue from positioning you as an expert in your field while supplying your contact details to several thousand potential customers.

Writing articles is hard work and time consuming. If you've been successful in getting an article published by one publication you should try and leverage it by approaching other similar organisations. You need to be careful here because no two publications would be keen to publish the exact same article. So if you're going to try and sell it to other media you need to make a number of changes. The most important change would be the headline. Then you might consider changing the order and maybe using different pictures. You just need to make it seem cosmetically different without having to re-invent the wheel.

Having put so much effort into your article, you want to make sure that you get the most value out of it.

Newspaper articles make excellent direct marketing pieces. See if the paper either has spare copies they don't need or will do you a reprint. These can then be sent out to your database. Alternatively you could email it to your contacts as a PDF. Newspaper articles also look great on your web site.

Trojan Horse

If you're not familiar with the term, you may well be wondering what I'm talking about now.

A Trojan Horse is basically a product or a service that you can either give away for free or in some very beneficial form which will attract potential customers.

We all know that Free is the most powerful word in sales and marketing, rivalled probably only by the word Sex.

The great thing about the word Free is that it gains attention. In all your marketing communications, the first thing you have to do is get your readers' attention. Free will do that. We also know that people can be persuaded to buy something solely to get the free item. There have been numerous times when I've bought a different Sunday newspaper because of the free film or CD being offered. Now in this instance the newspaper will make a heavily reduced margin on this one transaction. What they have done is a sampling exercise. Of the people who brand switch to get the free item, a percentage will decide they like the new paper and will become regular readers.

So what you need to do is look at your business and identify what your Trojan Horse might be. If you're a professional service business, could you give away a free consultation or a free report? If you're a retailer do you have a free item that you can afford to give away?

Once you have found a powerful Trojan Horse, all your marketing efforts become turbo charged.

The message should be prominently displayed on your web site, in any advertising, direct marketing, e-marketing or whatever channels you use.

Joint Ventures

Traditional marketing can be expensive. In tough economic times many companies will struggle to afford the expense.

The solution is to team up with appropriate synergistic businesses in joint ventures.

So what is a joint venture? It's when two or more companies work together for their mutual benefit – promoting both businesses simultaneously.

Classic examples of joint ventures (or strategic alliances as they're also called) are when one company piggy backs on another company's mail out. So say company A is sending out a communication to their customers. Company B will put their literature in with it so saving themselves the cost of the mail out. In this instance company B may then pay company A a percentage of the profit they make from the exercise or they may simply decide to share the mailing costs.

Another simple joint venture approach would be to place a link or information about one company's services on another company's web site. If this is accompanied by a bespoke special offer the uptake could be accurately monitored. Joint ventures work best if there is synergy between the two companies. For example if a dental practice mails its clients to remind them they are due an appointment, a company offering dental insurance would be a natural partner.

Joint ventures work especially well if the guest company makes a special offer tailored to the host company's customers. So in the dentist example, if the insurer were to offer a special discount to the patients of the dental practice, you have a win win situation. The insurer gets good uptake due to the accuracy of the targeting and the relevance of the offer and the dentist gets the good will created by their patients receiving a bespoke special offer.

When you're setting up a joint venture there are a few guidelines you're well advised to follow:

▶ Make sure your joint venture partner's image reflects well on your business.

▶ Companies with similar customer demographics to yours are likely to give you the best results.

▶ Both sides must have a clear understanding of how the host company will be remunerated before the activity kicks off.

Stay In Touch

This is so basic you would think it hardly needs saying but you'd be amazed how many companies only contact their customers when they're actually trying to sell them something or they're sending a bill.

Business is all about relationships. The more you're in touch with your customers the more opportunity you have to build the relationship.

There are all sorts of reasons for you to contact your customers:

▶ To communicate special offers
▶ To tell them their order has been dispatched
▶ To thank them for an order
▶ To inform them of new products and services
▶ To tell them about new developments in your company
▶ To check that they're happy with all aspects of your service
▶ To pass on industry news, trends and developments
▶ Their birthday/anniversary etc
▶ To offer them hospitality

The list is virtually endless. The whole point is to keep your company top of mind and to develop a reputation for excellent customer service.

With regard to the method of communication, that is entirely up to you. Whether you used the telephone, email, letter or social media is for you to decide.

Strategy 7: The Internet

The internet has only been around as the mass communication tool we all know since the mid nineties, but in that time it has totally changed many aspects of business and this trend is only going to increase.

From being a luxury just a few years ago, a high quality web site is now an absolute necessity. When we are approached by a new company the first thing we do is check them out online. If their web site is bad, or even worse, if they don't have a web site at all, it will have a dramatic impact on our likelihood of doing business with them.

It is estimated that there are in the region of 600 million web sites on the internet these days and that figure is still rapidly increasing. So you see why you have to work hard to make yours stand out.

While this can all sound a bit daunting, the internet provides massive opportunities for those companies who make the effort to get it right.

Two Step Process

There are two distinct jobs involved in making your web site the business generating machine you'd like it to be:

Firstly: you've got to get visitors to your site

Secondly: you've got to convert them into customers

Driving Traffic To Your Web Site

Probably the number 1 way of getting visitors to your web site these days is Pay Per Click advertising, of which Google Adwords is the dominant player.

For those of you who aren't familiar with Pay Per Click, these are the ads displayed at the top of the page and down the right hand side.

Pay per click in some ways is the marketing holy grail. Through your choice of key words and geographical selection your advertisement will be shown to only those people who are looking for what you sell. But it gets even better. You only pay when people actually click on your ad and go to your web site. Not only that but you decide how much you pay by the amount you bid for your keywords. Compare this with traditional newspaper advertising, where you pay a set amount and a large proportion of readers never see your ad and probably aren't interested in what you've got to sell anyway.

Setting Up A PPC Campaign

There are two ways to set up your campaign.

You can either do it yourself or you can employ one of the thousands of internet marketing companies. But be warned. Many of these so called "experts" are only one page ahead of you in the instruction book and may charge you unjustifiable amounts of money for their services.

If you plan to do it yourself but don't know where to start, the best idea is to use the Google online tutorial which will give you a basic introduction. The glory of this system is that a complete novice can have a PPC campaign running in a very short space of time. Your first stab at it may not be perfect but remember – if no one clicks on your advert it won't cost you a penny. Having established your campaign you can tweak it and refine it at a later date.

Use Traditional Offline Methods

Many businesses view their web site as a completely separate entity, divorced from the rest of their marketing materials. However the clever ones realise that traditional and digital media can work synergistically together to mutual benefit. It makes sense therefore to use your offline media to promote your online presence as your web site allows visitors to visit those pages which are especially relevant to them. All your traditional printed materials should encourage visits to your website.

Converting Visitors To Customers

This is of course the vital element of your internet marketing. There is little point in having 1000 visitors to your site if none of them become customers at any stage.

Research shows us we have somewhere between 5 – 10 seconds to grab our visitors' attention otherwise they'll be off to the next site. This highlights the importance of both the appearance and the content of your site.

The first thing to say is that you need to be realistic in your expectations. The chance of someone visiting your site and being so impressed that they become a customer on the first visit are very remote. Instead you should view your web site as a means of collecting names and email addresses so that you can build a relationship with them.

So how do you persuade them to give you their name and contact details?

The answer is by giving them the opportunity to apply for something of value that they want, such as a report, a white paper or a special offer. Once you have their name and e-mail address you can start regularly sending them useful and informative articles and information. This should, over time, establish your credentials as an authority and expert in your field so that at a later date when they do need your services, they already have a name and contact they trust. Your chances of then gaining them as a customer are hugely increased.

Some Website Tips

- ✓ Keep your site simple. Too many bells and whistles will put visitors off. People like to be able to see what they're looking for in a clear, logical and easily navigable format. Flashing lights and sound effects tend to confuse people who will vote with their fingers and be off to someone else's site.

- ✓ A website is like any other piece of communication. It needs a headline on each page to hook the reader in and take them into the body copy.

  You then keep their interest by spelling out the problems they face and how your product can solve them.

- ✓ You must make it easy for them to contact you. Every page should carry your contact details – phone number and e-mail address.

- ✓ Website visitors tend to skim read. So keep sentences short, use plenty of sub heads and bulleted lists.

- ✓ It's not all about you – it's about your visitors finding solutions to their problems. So make sure you don't just talk about your 20 years experience and how you started the business. Instead address their concerns and your solutions.

- ✓ Use testimonials on your home page as well as on a dedicated page. You can never have too many testimonials as they provide social proof that other people value what you do.

- ✓ Make your site interactive so that visitors can get involved with it. Have sign-up boxes for reports, newsletters and special offers.

✓ Make sure your site has plenty of value. If visitors find it a valuable information source then they are likely to come back. Include downloadable articles on subjects of interest to your visitors.

✓ One of the ways to add value to your site is to include special offers. For a retailer that could be a price discount or a 3 for 2 offer while for a consultancy business that could be a free initial consultation.

✓ Include a Resources page on which you list other relevant but non competing companies with links to their web sites. The point of this is to set up reciprocal links so that the other companies' sites carry links to your site. In bound links from relevant sites are one of the best ways to improve your website's positioning on the search engines.

✓ Create a blog. Not only does a blog position you as an expert in your field, someone who leads opinion on relevant topics but the search engines like blogs and are likely to reward you with enhanced page ranking.

✓ Review the content of your website regularly. It is very common for companies to create their website and then heave a huge sigh of relief that they can tick that job off. Content dates very fast and if your information isn't up to date your site will not be working as hard for you as it could be. Again search engines like new content and this will also help your page ranking.

✓ Include a brief video. If a visitor can see that the video only lasts 60 – 90 seconds they are very likely to click on it. The subject matter can either be you giving a very rapid overview of the benefits you can deliver to your customers or it could be a customer singing your praises in a testimonial. If you are speaking on the video this immediately starts to create a personality for your company and to build the first stage of a relationship with the visitor. Short videos are cheap and easy to produce these days and yes, you guessed it, search engines like video.

Strategy 8: Copywriting

How To Write Powerful Words That Sell

So far we have discussed a range of different marketing tools and approaches to help you grow and develop your business. Whatever approaches you choose, the vital common denominator will be the words you use.

What is it that differentiates a really good salesman from an average one? While things like empathy and personality are very important, the key will be in the words he uses and the arguments he puts forward. In print the salesman's personality isn't part of the equation, the full onus falls on the words themselves and the way the sales message is presented.

Some people are naturally good writers while others may find it more difficult. If you fall into the latter camp, don't worry. You can learn to be a good and persuasive copywriter.

While copywriting is an essentially creative process, there is an established formula you need to adhere to.

AIDCA

A **stands for ATTENTION.** The very first thing your copy must do is grab the reader's attention. In a lot of promotional literature therefore the headline has the job of getting the reader's attention. While it might sound a bit obvious, the headline has got to produce enough interest to persuade the reader to read on into the body copy. The headline is the front door of your communication through which your readers will come.

Questions work well in headlines. You are speaking directly to the reader and assuming that your targeting is accurate, you should be asking them a question which is directly relevant to them.

In newspapers, headlines have to work even harder. This is the reason why the tabloids have such lurid headlines. Newspapers are normally merchandised together in a newsagent so each headline is fighting against all the others. If the headline can attract someone's attention and interest there is a good chance that they will select that paper as opposed to one with a less engaging headline.

It is estimated that five times more people read a headline than read the rest of the copy which shows unfortunately that too many headlines don't do their job properly!

I stands for **INTEREST.** So assuming your headline has done a good enough job to attract attention, you've now got to interest your reader. Hit him with your best shot straight away. Give him the biggest benefits you have. Remember the difference between features and benefits. Talk the language of benefits – spelling out what your product will do for him.

Some writers like to keep their best stuff for the end – to finish on a high. This is misguided thinking. Some of your audience won't get as far as the end of your copy. The more benefits you give them early on, the more interested they'll be and the more chance that they'll read the whole piece.

D stands for **DESIRE.** Your readers have got to really want whatever it is you're selling. Hopefully all the benefits you've listed have created lots of interest, you've now got to really make them want what you're offering.

A classic way of creating desire is through using special offers.

C stands for **CONVICTION.** I've been interested by your benefits and your special offer has created plenty of desire but I'm not convinced. I don't know you. How do I know that your product is as good as you tell me it is? At the moment all the risk sits with me. I need to be convinced. Here is where our good friend from the Marketing Fundamentals section, the Guarantee, comes in. If you now give me some kind of guarantee that minimises my risk I may be convinced.

A stands for **ACTION.** So I've gone all through your copy and I'm pretty convinced. But you know how it is, I've got other things on my mind and perhaps I'll respond later. You need to include a call to action. You need the words which tell me to pick up the phone, come into your shop or click on the shopping button. Whatever action you want me to take, you need to tell me to do it now as opposed to coming back to it at some later stage.

So that's the theory of how you construct your communications but you've now got to actually get down and get the writing done.

Here are some guidelines to help you through the process:

1. **Set Your Objectives**

   Decide what you want your sales copy to achieve. This could be the number of sales you need, the number of leads you want to generate or the number of requests for more information. It doesn't matter what your objectives are, it's just useful to know in advance what you want.

2. **Understand Your Audience**

   The secret of successful copy is to talk your audience's language and to provide the benefits they are looking for. The only way you can do this is to know and to understand your audience.

   ☐ Is this business to business or business to consumer?

   ☐ Are you talking to men or women or both?

   ☐ How old are your audience?

   ☐ What are the demographics?

   ☐ Are they local or spread around the country?

   ☐ What business sectors are they in?

   ☐ What are the issues they face?

3. **Know Your Product And Its Benefits**

   Make sure you know everything about the subject you're writing about. Whether it's a product or a service you must have a full understanding of what it can do and the benefits it delivers to its customers. You should also have an understanding of the broader market place and any new developments within it.

4. **Work Out Your Structure**

   You need to decide how you're going to structure your communication. What information you are going to have in which section of the piece – what your special offer will be, will you include a guarantee and if so what form that will take and how you want people to respond.

The AIDCA format should make this process fairly easy.

You must also decide on your writing style. Will you write in a formal style or will you adopt a light, chatty approach? The answer to this is likely to be determined by your audience and to a degree on the type of product you're selling.

5. Experiment With Headlines

As we've already discussed the headline is probably the most important single element of your copy. If your headline doesn't make an impact then your readers won't get as far as the body copy.

You should try and write several headlines. It's amazing the difference a small tweak to a headline can make to the response rate. Write a number of headlines, some very similar and some very different and then review them later. Don't worry if you choose one initially and then change your mind. If you can get other people to give their opinions it will also help.

Headlines that make emotional appeals generally outsell those based on logic. Headlines that create pictures in readers' heads often help people to visualise and understand the benefits involved.

Asking questions in your headline has the effect of making readers think you're talking directly to them. "Do you want to give up smoking?", "Do you want to lose weight?"Both of these talk directly to these specified audiences and makes your communication directly relevant to them.

"How to..." is another highly effective way to start a headline, as it appears to offer the solution to a problem the reader may have. We've all seen the old favourite "How to lose 2 stone in a month". For those people who want to lose weight this is an irresistible headline.

There are plenty of other words which work powerfully in headlines. As I said earlier Free is probably the most powerful and persuasive word of all.

"You" means that you are talking directly to your reader.

"Introducing" indicates that you have something new, something the reader hasn't seen before.

"Did you know" tells me that you're going to tell me something interesting and maybe shocking.

"Compare" means you have something demonstrably better than I have currently.

6. **Use Testimonials**

   The purpose of your copy is to present your product in a way that persuades your readers that they want whatever it is you're selling. This means that you are going to sing its praises. You're going to fill your copy full of benefits and tell them that it is the best product for them.

   But you would say that wouldn't you.

   It's your product and you want to sell it.

   So the reader may well read your copy with a jaundiced eye, very aware that they're being sold to.

   This is where testimonials come in. A third party saying how good your product is and how it's benefited them is much more persuasive. So make sure you have testimonials from a few of your happy customers in your text.

   But as a cynical reader how do I know you haven't made the testimonial up. Well to be honest I can never really be sure but if you put a name, a job title and a company name if it's a B to B product or at least a name and town if it's a B to C item, then it becomes much more credible. Obviously this level of endorsement increases dramatically if the testimonial comes from a well known name or even a celebrity and the ultimate in testimonials comes when you include a photograph.

Too many companies include testimonials and ascribe them to Mrs S Brighton or Mr W Northampton. This type of testimonials add very little as consumers are rightly sceptical.

One word of warning however is to make sure that you've got agreement from your customers to use their testimonials. If you overlook this you may end up alienating and so losing some of your best customers.

Make Your Readers Take Action

When you write sales copy there is only one result you're looking for. You want people to take action and buy what you're selling. But we know how difficult it is to overcome inertia. Even if your readers are interested, there is a great tendency to put off doing anything. What you need them to do is to take action and respond to the offer you're making them.

The crucial point here is that you must make a clear and simple offer that compels the reader to respond. There are two key elements in what I've just said:

1. Only have one offer. With one offer your readers will clearly understand exactly your proposition. If you include more than one offer you run the risk of confusing your message and so confusing your readers. The result will be a lower response level.
2. Make your offer as strong as possible. Not surprisingly the stronger the offer, the greater the response level.

So your copy has communicated lots of lovely benefits and made your readers an irresistible offer but you now need them to take that vital step and do something about it. You must make it as simple as possible for them to respond and the instructions should be spelt out in easy to follow terms. Repeating the call to action a few times through your communication will also increase your response rate as different people will be ready to respond at different stages of the communication.

There are of course lots of ways to respond and you must decide what form you want your responses to come in.

- ▶ Call 1234 56789 today
- ▶ Bring this coupon into our shop today
- ▶ Go to our website www.ourbizz.co.uk and fill in your details
- ▶ Return the reply paid card to take advantage of our offer

Another way to increase response is to time limit your offer or to put a limit on the number of special items available.

- ✓ Take advantage of our fantastic special offer today. Offer closes 31st March
- ✓ Offer limited to the first 200 respondents

Polish Your Copy

Having done a first draft, leave it for a while. Whether that's an hour or a day is up to you. When you come back to it, your head will be clear and you can read it dispassionately. If you're anything like me you will almost certainly make lots of changes.

When you review it, check for the following:

- ✓ Have you understood your audience and addressed their concerns?
- ✓ Have you really focused on the benefits or are there still too many features?
- ✓ Will your readers see what's in it for them?
- ✓ Is your language appropriate?
- ✓ Is the copy easy on the eye or does it look a bit daunting?

✓ Have you broken the text up with sub heads and bullet points?

✓ Is it the right length? I'll talk about this a bit more in a moment

✓ Is the offer strong enough to create real desire?

✓ Is there still too much risk for a new customer?

✓ Is there a loud call to action and is it really clear what the reader should do next?

Long Copy vs Short Copy

This is a perennial favourite. There is a general perception that no one will ever be bothered to read long copy. Many times clients have said to me that they don't want direct marketing copy to be more than one page long.

The fact is that long copy will outsell short copy every time as long as you've got other parts of the activity right.

The reason for this is simple. Long copy gives you much more opportunity to spell out the benefits of whatever you're selling but your reader has to be interested in what you're saying. So it comes down to your targeting. If you're talking to the wrong person, whether the copy is long or short won't matter as the reader won't be interested. Whereas if your targeting is right and the copy is relevant and interesting to the reader then they will read everything you give them.

If for example you were writing about some gardening product, if you target teenage girls, the chances are they won't be interested so whether you write one page or five pages is irrelevant. However if you have a list of opted in members from a garden centre mailing list, they will probably be interested in every word you write.

Check, Check And Check Again

Personally speaking I find nothing more irritating than getting direct communications with mistakes in them – spelling mistakes, grammatical mistakes or whatever. If they can't make their communication error free, what chance is there that their service will be any better.

So at this stage you now need to go through your text with a fine tooth comb. The best place to start is with the spell checker, although you must remember that this will often give you American spellings. Once you've done this, I advise you to print the text out. It seems to be much easier to check words in hard copy than on a screen and it also allows you to write in any amends you want to make.

After you've checked the spelling and the grammar, review the flow. Does each point follow on logically from the point before? Is there a logical progression through the text? Have you followed the AIDCA model and is` interest and involvement maintained throughout?

If you can answer yes to all these points, you should have a powerful and effective selling machine in your hands.

A Reminder Of Copywriting Basics

✓ Don't use long, clever words. Use simple, basic language that anyone can understand.

✓ Use short, sharp sentences. Readers will get confused by long convoluted sentences.

✓ Don't be clever and cryptic. Copywriting is not the time to show off.

✓ Write in the language appropriate to your audience. You're not looking for a literature prize so don't get hung up about grammatical correctness.

✓ Engage your readers' emotions and paint verbal pictures for them.

✓ Focus on the benefits the product will deliver to your audience.

✓ Don't worry about the length of your copy but don't waffle. Each word must justify its place in your text but as long as your targeting is good and your information is relevant, then your readers will read as much as you give them.

✓ Include testimonials.

✓ Use time limited special offers.

✓ Always use easily understood calls to action.

✓ Give as many ways to respond as possible.

✓ In a sales letter include a PS to summarise the benefits.

Strategy 9: Direct Mail

How To Run Campaigns Which Turn Readers Into Buyers

The last tool we discussed was copywriting and how to make your copy a powerful sales tool. It makes sense to follow that by looking at another vital tool in the business development armoury – direct mail, in which copy is a key element.

Just to be absolutely clear, when I refer to direct mail I am talking about sending letters through the post to named individuals. I'm not talking about e-mail marketing, although some of the guidelines would be relevant to e-mail marketing.

Now we're all aware of direct mail or junk mail as it is sometimes referred to. Unfortunately done badly, it fully deserves the title. The way a lot of direct mail is done, the letter that is sent out has as much value to the recipient as junk and the bin is the right place for it to end up.

The purpose of this section is to give you the relevant guidance and weaponry to make sure that your direct mail campaigns give you a great ROI and generate loads of hot prospects. Be in no doubt, direct mail, even though a lot of marketing people these days look down their nose at it, can, if done well, be a great way of growing your business.

What Are Your Objectives?

The objectives of your direct mail campaign will differ from business to business. You may want:

► To generate immediate sales

► A request for more information or a sales visit

► A visit to a web site

► A telephone call

Whatever method you choose, your sole objective is to get the recipients to respond to you in some way.

To have any chance of getting a response (except telling you never to communicate with them again) there are three separate elements that you have to get right.

1. You have to communicate with a carefully identified and targeted audience.
2. Your letter must contain a compelling offer, directly relevant to that particular niche audience.
3. The letter must be presented and written in a persuasive enough manner to make them take action.

Target Your Letter

The effectiveness of your direct mail campaign will be determined by the relevance of what you're offering to the recipients of the letter. If you send an offer relating to football to an audience of elderly women, it is unlikely that the campaign will be successful. However if you sent them a letter making them a great offer on (forgive the stereotyping) embroidery materials or flower arranging, you are much more likely to be successful.

So the first basic rule is that you must know the profile of the users of your product. Now all you need to do is get your hands on a list of these people.

So the question is how can I get hold of a suitable list?

The answer is that your list can come from a variety of sources

1. Your own database. Depending on how you have segmented your list you should have a list of customers – people who have bought before. These will of course be the most fertile list you will ever find and should give you a very high conversion rate.

    You may well also have a list of lapsed users – customers who have stopped buying from you. This group should be relatively easy to convert as they have bought before but for some reason have drifted away. The right offer should give you excellent results.

    You may also have a list of leads who you have never converted. At some stage this group showed an interest in your product so again the right offer should provide good conversion levels.

2. Bought lists. There are any number of list brokers out there, all desperate to sell you names and addresses. The quality of this kind of list will depend on:

a. The accuracy of your buyer's profile. If you can define accurately the profile of your prospects, you should be able to buy a list which closely conforms to the profile.

b. The quality of your list broker. If you can find a high quality list broker with access to specialist lists who is willing to work hard to match your buyer's profile to appropriate lists, again you should get a good result.

3. Joint venture partners. We've talked earlier about joint ventures. The trick is to find a non competitive partner who serves the same audience. An example of this might be a commercial stationers doing a joint venture with an office furniture company or a company providing serviced offices. So you tap in to the partner's database, either piggy backing on activity they're doing or simply using their database and maybe paying them a percentage of all sales generated.

How To Get Your Letter In Front Of Your Audience

Following the copywriting section, hopefully you can put together a compelling letter, filled with benefits, an irresistible offer, social proof in the form of customer testimonials and a risk reversal guarantee. But it doesn't matter how well crafted your letter is, if your prospects don't actually read it.

So what can you do to get your letter into the right hands, opened and read?

a. **Don't make your direct mail look like direct mail.** When you receive a glossy envelope with a corporate logo on the outside, you know you're about to be sold to. These letters often don't get opened and just get thrown away. It amazes me that plenty of large corporates continue to throw their money down the drain in this way.

b. **Use an ordinary envelope and hand write the address.** This is very time consuming but does make it look like a personal letter. If you feel this will take too long and there is no one else you can cheaply rope in to do it, the next best is to print directly onto the envelope.

c. **Don't frank the letter.** Franking is something only done by companies so again I know in advance that I'm about to be sold to. The answer is to use stamps. Again this makes the letter look like a personal communication.

d. **Make the envelope bulky.** If you enclose something in the envelope, the recipient is bound to be curious. Bulky mail is invariably opened. Clever marketers now make sure that whatever they have included has some relevance either to whatever they're offering or is at least referenced in the offer. Traditionally the link can be a bit cheesy. Including a piece of chewing gum which is then referred to in the letter "Here's an offer you might like to chew over." A tube of glue with the line " You'll never be stuck for ideas again." Bulky mail gives you the opportunity to get creative. It's number one objective is to get the letter opened but it has so much more impact if you can link the object thematically to your offer or at least make the recipient smile.

e. **Use non traditional envelopes.** If you send your letter in a poster tube, virtually everyone will be curious to find out what's inside. If you use an A4 envelope instead of a standard DL, it no longer looks like a traditional piece of direct mail.

Make Them Take Action

Irrespective of how well you've executed all these points, you're still only going to get a finite level of response.

So how can you increase the response levels?

a. **Personalise your letter.** How big a turn off is it to receive a letter addressed to "The Householder" or Dear Sir/Madam or even "The Premium Buyer." All of these salutations tell you that the sender hasn't taken the trouble to really work at their targeting. They are probably "spraying and praying." They've just got a generic list and thrown out thousands of letters with no real attention to the relevance of the offer to the recipients. However when I get a letter addressed "Dear Mr Jennings", I know I'm being sold to but at least I'll go to the second line.

b. **Include a voucher.** If you're offering a discount – either a set amount ie "£10 off" or a percentage "Save 20%," by including a voucher, which actually feels like money, you give the offer a real sense of value.

c. **Time limit your offer.** I've already mentioned this but if you put a closing date on the offer, whether that's a discount or a BOGOF (buy one, get one free) your redemption rate will go up dramatically. Without the closing date people feel they can redeem it any time, put it off and end up never redeeming it at all.

Strategy 10: Information Products

How To Use Them To Generate A Flow Of Leads

I've placed a lot of emphasis on leads as they are usually the starting point for new business. I've already talked about several ways to generate leads and in this chapter I'm going to focus on how to use information products to generate warm, pre-qualified leads. Let's be honest, how much easier is it to work with prospects who have already demonstrated that they are interested in what you have to sell as opposed to having to knock on completely new doors.

The other thing about creating an information product is how it positions you in the market. If you have written a book or produced a CD, then you must be an expert because only an expert would have the knowledge and gravitas to write a book, to become an author.

And if you're an expert in your field, then surely you will charge a premium price. And if you charge a premium price then you must be an expert.

What a fantastic circular argument.

Leverage Your Experience

It's often said that there is a book in all of us. When you actually think of your knowledge and expertise there are probably several books in most of us. It's this expertise that other people would like to get their hands on and will often be prepared to pay good money to do so.

The thinking behind this tried and tested strategy is to offer your knowledge and experience as a way of generating qualified leads.

What you have to remember is that you don't necessarily get paid for what you do, but for what you've done. Think about that for a moment. It's your experience that people want to take advantage of.

So What Are You Going To Create?

Information products can come in a variety of formats:

- ▶ Book
- ▶ Booklet
- ▶ Downloadable PDF
- ▶ DVD
- ▶ CD
- ▶ MP3

You can choose to produce your product in physical form, but this obviously has cost implications or you can create it electronically for your prospects to download.

Whichever route you go down, you will want to exchange your product for your prospect's contact details. Once you have their contact details and you know that they are interested in whatever topic your product is about, you have a warm, qualified lead.

Creating Your Information Product

1. **The Theme**

   What is the overall theme of your book?(or whatever format you've decided on). For the sake of this chapter, let's assume you're producing a book. What is it going to be about? You obviously need to select a topic on which you are an expert. In most cases this will be some aspect of your core business. So whether that's about business development, dry cleaning or pet grooming it doesn't matter. As long as you know where to find an audience, people will be keen to benefit from your expertise.

2. **The Title**

   Selecting a title is an absolutely vital part of the process. Before you start you must be clear about your audience so that the title will be suitable for your prospective readers. Your choice of words and tone of voice will be different if you are talking to solicitors as opposed to pregnant mothers or students.

   If your title is bland or boring, people are not going to be attracted to it. This is where you have to be creative. You need to find a sparky, intriguing and engaging title which stands out and grabs the interest of your audience.

   There are a number of approaches which do just that:

   ☐ Tips on what to do or what not to do

   ☐ The mistakes that should be avoided

   ☐ The steps you need to take

These approaches will lead to titles that start like these:

7 things you need to know about...

21 shocking statistics ...

10 steps to...

When creating your title jot down anything and everything that comes into your head. At this stage don't start editing or being critical of your efforts. Your wackiest creation may be the best. Once you've created your list, show them to colleagues or friends and see which ones they like. The key here is that a good title will guarantee interest and uptake in your audience while an uninspired title that doesn't capture the imagination will flop.

3. **Topics To Include**
   What are the topics you want to include in the book? For topics here you can read chapters. So what are the main subjects that you're going to cover off? The same rules will apply to your book as apply to a direct mail letter. You have to make sure that each section is interesting enough for the reader to keep reading. So kick off with your big guns. Your first chapter should contain big ideas in order to hook your readers in.

4. **The Content**
   Having decided what the main subject areas are, now you have to work out what the detailed content of each chapter will be.

   The best way to do this is to plan it out on paper. You start with the overall theme, under that you write your snappy and intriguing title, then each chapter and then the detailed content.

   At this stage you must be sure that the order and flow are right. Get the chapters in the right order and then the content of each chapter so there is a logical flow and progression. Having done this once take a break and come back and do it again. Very often you will make changes when you go through it the second time.

5. **Writing The Words**
That's the planning stage done. Now comes the real work. Actually sitting down and writing the book.

The best advice here is to write it as if you were talking to a friend. The style should be conversational, light and chatty.

Why write like this? Because no one wants to wade through stuffy, turgid prose. You want your readers to enjoy the experience, which they will if it feels as if you are having a one to one conversation with them.

The first section you'll have to write will be the introduction. A good way to start is with either the word "of" or "because."

❝Of all the books you could have chosen to read today, I'm very pleased you chose this one...❞

❝Because you're reading this introduction, I know that growing your business is something you're interested in❞

This kind of approach will immediately hook the reader in.

You will also have to write your biography, which allows the reader to see your track record and understand why he should take notice of what you say. Including a picture of yourself isn't vanity, it allows the reader to establish more of a relationship with you.

The last bits you'll need are a price, because that gives the book a value and positions your work as valuable. When you then use it for marketing purposes, it becomes something people actually want. Your prospects will make an effort to get their hands on your marketing tool.

Similarly a bar code and ISBN code confirms the status of your book as a serious work which you might well find in a book shop or your local library.

Marketing Your Book

Now you have to decide how you're going to market your book and of course there are lots of mechanics you can use:

- ✓ E-marketing
- ✓ Social Media
- ✓ Advertisements
- ✓ Direct mail
- ✓ Flyers
- ✓ Inserts

Whatever methods you choose, you need to generate enough interest to generate a response. You will want to drive them to a web page because you have to collect, as a minimum, their name, email address and phone number. You may also want to learn a bit about their business, but the basic contact information will make up the mandatory fields.

So they give you their contact details and now they are able to either download the book or you send it to them in the post.

Following Up

Now comes the bit where you turn a prospect into a lead. You already know that they are interested in whatever it is you have to sell so your conversion rate should be good.

So the next and crucial stage is for you to phone them up. Whether you're selling a service or a product, your objective now is to arrange a meeting. In your conversation you must make it very clear that you will be actively selling at the meeting. Offering something such as a one hour consultancy session for free may make it easier to get the appointment. Whatever technique you use, this is the culmination of all the work you've put in and hopefully will be the start of a long term relationship.

In Summary

You now have a 10 step plan which will enable you to take your business to wherever you want it to go.

It's now down to you to actually make it happen. History is littered with businesses which never reached their potential because either the business owner never got his act together to market and promote his business effectively or never had the confidence to make a start.

Now is the time to be bold. Making a mistake isn't a crime. The crime is never trying. Almost every successful entrepreneur will admit to making masses of mistakes but they regard these mistakes as learning opportunities. As long as you learn from your mistakes, you'll do it better the next time.

So take your courage in both hands and start building yourself the successful business you always dreamed of.

I wish you every success.

Mike

Webliography...

The following websites contain useful information to help you grow and develop your business.

Advertising

- ▶ www.adassoc.org.uk

Business Help

- ▶ www.entrepreneur.com
- ▶ www.morebusiness.com
- ▶ www.smallbusiness.co.uk
- ▶ www.startups.co.uk
- ▶ www.businesslink.gov.uk

Blogging

- ▶ www.blogger.com
- ▶ www.wordpress.com

Copywriting

- ▶ www.copywriting.co.uk
- ▶ www.copyblogger.com

E payment

- ▶ www.paypal.com
- ▶ www.paypoint.net

Exhibitions

- ▶ www.exhibitions.co.uk

Internet Marketing

- ▶ www.buydomains.com
- ▶ www.searchEngineWatch.com

Mailing lists

- ▶ www.marketingfile.com

Marketing

- ▶ www.cim.co.uk

Market Research

- ▶ www.marketresearchworld.net

Marketing Services

- ▶ www.mch.co.uk

Networking

- ► www.bni.com
- ► www.4networking.biz

PR

- ► www.prca.org.uk

Sales Promotion

- ► www.theipm.org.uk
- ► www.marketingteacher.com

Social Networking

- ► www.ecademy.com
- ► www.facebook.com
- ► www.linkedin.com
- ► www.twitter.com

Notes...

10 Essential Business Strategies

10 Essential Business Strategies

BDA

Business Development Advisors

www.businessdevelopmentadvisors.co.uk